All-American Fighting Forces

★ ★ ★

AMERICAN INDIAN CODE TALKERS

★ ★ ★

JULIA GARSTECKI

BLACK
RABBIT
BOOKS

Bolt is published by Black Rabbit Books
P.O. Box 3263, Mankato, Minnesota, 56002.
www.blackrabbitbooks.com
Copyright © 2017 Black Rabbit Books

Design and Production by Michael Sellner
Photo Research by Rhonda Milbrett

Library of Congress Control Number: 2015954840

HC ISBN: 978-1-68072-003-7   PB ISBN: 978-1-68072-284-0

Printed in the United States at CG Book Printers,
North Mankato, Minnesota, 56003. PO #1794 4/16

Web addresses included in this book were working and appropriate
at the time of publication. The publisher is not responsible for broken
or changed links.

Image Credits
Alamy: Everett Collection Inc,
Cover; Corbis: AS400 DB, 9; Berliner
Verlag/Archiv, 22–23 (background); Dream-
stime: Grey 18, 14; Zim235, 15 (top left); Flickr:
Normandie, 28–29 (background); Mathers Museum
of World Cultures: 6; mcu.usmc.mil: 26; Saunders, 12;
Sgt. Williams, 32; Newscom: Everett Collection, Back
Cover, 1, 19; JON FREEMAN/REX, 26; Shutterstock: Bob
Orsillo, 15 (top right); Jason Salmon, 28–29 (morse code
key); USMC: 4–5; Official Marine Corps Photo #QH-
CR67PZMRY4-180-15, 25; Official Marine Corps Photo
#QHCR67PZMRY4-180-17, 31; Official Marine Corps
Photo #QHCR67PZMRY4-180-19, 16–17; Official Ma-
rine Corps Photo #QHCR67PZMRY4-180-23, 3, 20;
Wikimedia: 10–11; Mark Pellegrini, 15 (bottom)
Every effort has been made to contact copyright
holders for material reproduced in this book.
Any omissions will be rectified in subse-
quent printings if notice is given
to the publisher.

Contents

CHAPTER 1

A  in World War I

Tired and dirty, U.S. soldiers tried to sneak up on the enemy. But wherever they went, enemies attacked. Spies were listening in on phone calls. The United States needed a secret code.

U.S. Soldiers
in World
War I

total soldiers
soldiers wounded
soldiers killed
prisoners of war

An Idea

One day, a **captain** heard soldiers talking in their Choctaw Indian language. That gave him an idea. He placed Choctaw soldiers with each army unit. They passed information to each other in their home language.

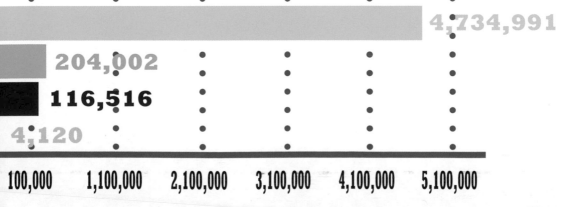

4,734,991

204,002

116,516

4,120

| 100,000 | 1,100,000 | 2,100,000 | 3,100,000 | 4,100,000 | 5,100,000 |

The First Code Talkers

The Choctaw soldiers became known as Code Talkers. Spies could not understand them. U.S. soldiers were able to surprise the enemy. Soon, the United States and its **allies** won World War I.

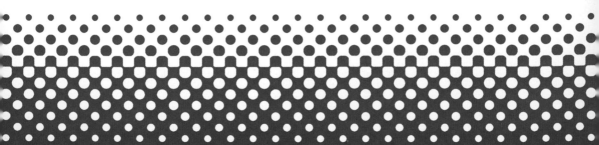

CHAPTER 2

Talkers in World War II

When World War II started, the military wanted to use Code Talkers again. The military asked American Indians to join. They had to know their **native** language and English.

11

Training

The American Indian soldiers trained. They learned to fight and use weapons. Then the Code Talkers went into special training. They learned to use the code.

Tribes of World War II Code Talkers

- ● Assiniboine
- ● Cherokee
- ● Chippewa
- ● Choctaw
- ● Comanche
- ● Hopi
- ● Kiowa
- ● Menominee
- ● Muscogee/Creek
- ● Navajo
- ● Oneida
- ● Pawnee
- ● Sac and Fox
- ● Seminole
- ● Sioux

Learning the Code

Native languages didn't have words for bombs or planes. So the Indian soldiers created a code. The code used everyday words to stand for battle gear. Their word for "whale" stood for "battleship." Learning the code took a lot of practice.

Tools for
Communication

CAMP PHONES

RADIOS

TELEGRAPHS

NOTEBOOKS

THE NAVAJO CODE

Code Talkers used everyday words to stand for military words.

English Navajo Code Word
What the Navajo Word Meant

battleship
lo-tso
whale

bomber plane
jay-sho
buzzard

America
ne-he-mah
our mother

bombs
a-ye-shi
eggs

submarine
besh-lo
iron fish

captain
besh-legai-nah-kih
two silver bars

cruiser
lo-tso-yazzie
small whale

destroyer
ca-lo
shark

The Navajo Indian language was used more than other native languages.

fighter plane
da-he-tih-hi
hummingbird

Germany
besh-be-cha-he
iron hat

CHAPTER 3

Using the

Code in Battle

Two Talkers went with each **regiment**. Three others stayed at **headquarters**. They used their codes to talk to each other. They reported any problems. They also used the code to tell soldiers where to go.

American Indian Soldiers in

WORLD WAR II
BY THE NUMBERS

5,000

number of
Indian soldiers
in 1941

more than
44,000
number of
Indian soldiers
in 1945

Dangerous Jobs

Code Talkers laid wire for radios and telephones. This job was dangerous. Sometimes enemies shot at them.

Code Talkers were also spies. They used the code to tell soldiers where enemies hid.

about 500
number of
WWII Code Talkers

AXIS

ALLIES

CHAPTER 4

Secret Work

During large attacks, Talkers directed where to send **supplies** and soldiers. They sent more than 800 messages in just a few days. The enemy never knew what they were saying.

The Talkers' job was very secret. They were not allowed to talk about their work. Many U.S. soldiers had no idea what Talkers did during the war.

Finally Celebrated

More than 50 years after the war, the Code Talkers were celebrated. The United States gave them medals for their work.

Code Talkers were smart, brave, and stayed calm during attacks. Their work saved many lives. And they helped win wars. Code Talkers were later used in two other wars. The code was never broken.

TIMELINE

JULY 1914

World War I begins.

OCTOBER 1918

Choctaw Indians become the first Code Talkers.

SEPTEMBER 1942

The Marine Corps creates the Navajo Code Talker program.

1914   1924   1934   1944   1954

NOVEMBER 1918

World War I ends.

DECEMBER 1941

The United States enters World War II.

1942-1945
Code Talkers help the United States win battles during the war.

NOVEMBER 2013
The U.S. Congress celebrates the American Indian Code Talkers.

1964   1974   1984   1994   2004   2014

SEPTEMBER 1945
World War II ends.

GLOSSARY

Allies (al-EYZ)—the United States, Great Britain, Soviet Union, France, and other countries that fought against Germany, Italy, and Japan during World War II

ally (AL-i)—a country that supports and helps another country in war

Axis (AK-ses)—the countries of Germany, Italy, and Japan during World War II

captain (KAP-ten)—an officer of high rank in the military

headquarters (HED-kwor-turz)—a place from which business or military action is directed

native (NAY-tiv)—belonging to a person since birth

regiment (RE-juh-muhnt)—a military unit that is made of several large groups of soldiers

supply (SUH-pli)—a thing, such as food or a weapon, that is needed for a particular purpose

BOOKS

Adams, Simon. *World War II.* Eyewitness Books. New York: DK Publishing, 2014.

Samuels, Charlie. *Spying and Security.* Redding, CT: Brown Bear Books, 2012.

Thompson, Ben. *Guts & Glory: World War II.* Guts and Glory. Boston: Little, Brown, and Company, 2016.

WEBSITES

Code Talkers
www.archives.gov/research/native-americans/ military/code-talkers.html

Navajo Code Talkers
navajocodetalkers.org

U.S. Navy Navajo Code
ww2db/other.php?other_id=29

INDEX